EVERY WOMAN'S
DICK-TIONARY

FOR *CHEATING*
MEN!

Note for Librarians: A cataloguing record for this book is available from Library and Archives Canada at www.collectionscanada.ca/amicus/index-e.html
ISBN 1-4120-8345-1

PUBLISHING

Offices in Canada, USA, Ireland and UK
This book was published *on-demand* in cooperation with Trafford Publishing. On-demand publishing is a unique process and service of making a book available for retail sale to the public taking advantage of on-demand manufacturing and Internet marketing. On-demand publishing includes promotions, retail sales, manufacturing, order fulfilment, accounting and collecting royalties on behalf of the author.

Book sales for North America and international:
Trafford Publishing, 6E–2333 Government St.,
Victoria, BC V8T 4P4 CANADA
phone 250 383 6864 (toll-free 1 888 232 4444)
fax 250 383 6804; email to orders@trafford.com
Book sales in Europe:
Trafford Publishing (UK) Limited, 9 Park End Street, 2nd Floor
Oxford, UK OX1 1HH UNITED KINGDOM
phone 44 (0)1865 722 113 (local rate 0845 230 9601)
facsimile 44 (0)1865 722 868; info.uk@trafford.com
Order online at:
trafford.com/06-0100

10 9 8

YOU REALLY LOVE YOUR MAN!
AND WANT THE RELATIONSHIP TO WORK... BUT NOT AT THE COST OF YOUR DIGNITY !!!

IF A RELATIONSHIP IS TO WORK, THOSE INVOLED MUST BE HONEST WITH EACH OTHER. WITH EACH PARTNER SHOULDERING HIS OR HER EQUAL SHARE OF BURDEN, LOVE AND COMMITMENT. ANYTHING OTHER WISE, AND YOU MIGHT AS WELL BE HONEST WITH YOURSELVES AND STOP WASTING EACH OTHERS TIME AND AGREE TO MOVE FORWARD....**SEPARATELY!**

101 WAYS TO KNOW IF YOUR MAN IS CHEATING ON YOU
THIS MANIFESTO WILL TAKE THE GUESS WORK OUT OF FIGURING OUT IF THE MAN YOU ARE WITH IS WORTH THE CONTINUING INVESTMENTS OF YOUR BODY, MIND AND SOUL.

HOW DO I DECEIVE THEE, LET ME COUNT THE WAYS....

#(16.) HE BUYS YOU FLOWERS FOR NO REASON......EXCEPT THAT HE'S FEELING GUILTY AS "HELL" FOR SLEEPING WITH YOUR BEST FRIEND!

STOP SECOND GUESSING YOURSELF, STOP WASTING YOUR TIME & STOP THE MERRY-GO-ROUND. IF YOUR RELATIONSHIP IS GOING IN CIRCLES......ORDER NOW!

Introduction

Well let's get started on who I am and what this Manifesto is all about. Can you spell "TRADER?" Because that's how I feel.

I am a retired MALE Playboy about to reveal all the Secrets of the Trade.

I take no pride in this revelation but let's call it a realization as to what I was and the mental carnage I have caused through the years to unsuspecting female suitors.

You may be asking yourself what if any credentials or expertise I may have relating to the topic of "Cheating Men." Let's just say I have a Ph.D. in womanizing and a Master's in making women do something that normally, their morals would forbid.

The omission of my real name is for obvious reasons: Maintaining life!!! Because I have committed the Worst of all SINS, Mutiny against the MALE RACE!

Now with that being said let the records show that this is my way of vindication for the wrongs I have committed, as well as for all other players, playboys, pimps, unfaithful boyfriends, cheating husbands, want to be lovers, **WOMAN BEATERS**, men without morals, child molesters, and any other sexual deviates that are against God's Morals.

Cheating men want to see how much fun they can have before they go to **HELL**. (Hint.) The more women they get, the more fun they have. Cheating men give equal opportunity to all women regardless of how they look. She could be so fat, that she has more chins than a Chinese telephone book. Cheating men don't care because they feel they never go to bed with an ugly woman, they just wake up with them.

Judgment Day has at last arrived for all Ye'ole Cheat'en Male Ho "Sinners" of Planet Earth.

(And theirs a lot of them.)

IT'S about time we put back some moral fiber into our society which time and Man has decayed to the point that as a civilization we perceive the image of women to be only a sexual object to serve man's fantasies and sexual desires.

This is perpetuated in every media there is. TV, movies, magazines, Internet, water cooler conversations, and things of the sort. This Manifesto will be a catalyst to bring back respect and integrity to all Women on planet Earth. The Serpent of Evil towards women will be unveiled and exposed to the TRUTH!

I'm going on somewhat of a tangent but you can feel the compassion and now resentment I have on the subject of "Cheating Men."

I will warn you in advance that the information I am about to reveal however politically incorrect it may be or on occasion unethical and possibly illegal, don't lose sight of the question?

Is your man cheating on you?

I'm sure you've heard of fight fire with fire, what's good for the goose is good for the gander, an eye for an eye, a tooth for a tooth, pay back, what goes around comes around, do unto others as they would do unto to you, I could go on but I think you get the message.

Since I'm on clichés, here are a few you might want to give some consideration to before you continue:

Let sleeping dogs lie! What you don't know can't hurt you! Ask me no questions and I'll tell you no lies! Don't step in shit and it won't stink!

The point here is that sometimes the truth does hurt, and fact is if you have bothered to order this Manifesto you are already in some form of doubt or denial.

Before getting started you must consider that the derogatory information you may find out could potentially wreck marriages, relationships and families. Not to mention the monetary and mental toll it may have on you.

As your Captain I will be blatantly honest, possibly hurting your feelings or even insulting you at times. However *"Stupidity"* is not a crime, so you're free to stop reading now!

For those of you who are emotionally dormant and mechanical like in your thinking and relationships. You will need verbal shock treatment to jump start your commonsense to see the LIGHT.....You will get that and much more in what's to come.

So if you feel any apprehension on what the following information may reveal: *STOP NOW !!!*

Your loss will only be the cost of this Manifesto, which is the lesser of two evils.

Before we get started keep in mind that this information gathered is from a man's perspective and at times may seem simple, obvious and condescending.

That's because men are primitive by nature and boy like. Allow me to elaborate more on the subject. Every time a man see's an attractive woman he regresses mentally back to the time when our ancestor's knuckles dragged the ground and their most basic instinct second to eating was copulation. Now all that muscle and bronze along with what little intellect he may have is reduced to lust with no strength to resist.

If you think about it, the sex act in itself is very animal like! I don't care how refined you are, how much education you have or how good you look. While in the act of sex you make unintelligible sounds, incomplete sentences, use bad grammar and use GOD'S name in vain. And that's just the verbal part.

DAMN! I don't know if that was good for you but it certainly put a tingle in my spine.

See! There I go. HELL I Can't Even Write about This WITHOUT Feeling like a HO!

Now Take a Moment. Relax; Go Get Yourself a DRINK OR SMOKE and Sit down and FASTSEN Your Seat Belts Because I'm going to Take You on a Roller Coaster Ride of EMOTIONS and TRUTH.

As I have taken over the bodies of so many women before, now I'm going to take over your MIND.

Pretend that I'm beaming you up mentally aboard a Vacation Cruise Ship.

I am your **CAPTAIN** preparing you to set sail on a journey of "**TRUTH.**" Once we leave the dock there's no turning back and I warn you that the waves of Truth can be Very High and **FURIOUS.**

Like the Titanic you could go down. As your **CAPTAIN**, I will try to keep you afloat.

So off we go. The seas are calm and the sky is blue with a soft warm wind blowing with the sweet and sour smell of the ocean. Accompanied by the echoing sounds of sea gulls in the distant blue-sky line.

As the sight of land wands to the east we now have embarked on a trip into the unknown. Lets call this day one and the following "**#WAYS**" are possible signs that your man is **<u>CHEATING!!!</u>**

DISCLAIMER

I would like to take this time to apologize for all the grammatical mistakes in the documents to follow. I decided against the judgment of my editors not to make corrections. Reasons being that I take the thesis of what I am presenting to be personal and serious. (However funny it may be at times.) I intentionally don't want to commercialize my writing. That's to say that I want my readers to feel the human side of what I'm writing. To be human is to error and it is through these errors that we define our lives. I am a man of little formal education, which I feel should be beside the point. I am reporting the truth as I know it in the best manner I can. So know what you read is real no matter how badly written it may be! And educate yourselves (For those of you who need it.) through the errors of others and yourself.

YOUR CAPTAIN

WAY# (1.)Any Changes From What You Feel Is Routine Or Normal

Such as: hanging out or going out with the fellows. Now let's put this in perspective. Most if not all men have friends that they spend time with. However if there were a sudden change in frequency and hours to there so-called hanging out with friends would be a clue.

When a man cheats, he needs an alibi. And what would be a more believable alibi and easy to say than I'm going out with the boy's. You may have raised eye-brows as to how obvious this is but keep in mind that were just getting started. Another example would be a sudden change in the time (ex-tended) he comes home from wherever he normally goes. The point here is to be with another woman takes time away from you and this is usually the first sign something is wrong. Cheating men will always exspose themselves by their actions, not their words.

WAY# (2.) The Sudden Announcement Of I'm Tired

Ladies, I know you can relate to this one. I'm tired, I don't feel good, I have a bad headache, or some part of your man's anatomy is hurting. However true, these statements may be at the time. It's just an excuse. Let me explain. Whether consciously or unconsciously when your Man makes this statement; "I'm tired." It really means I'm not up to having sex with you tonight. Once again this in itself is normal however, put this declaration with WAY# (1.) and you'll see a birth of what's to be a pattern. Now for those you who can't read between the lines, what your man is really saying; "I have just had sex with someone else and my performance was so outstanding that I don't have anything left for you." The flip side of this is that he could be planning to cheat on you the next day and wants his nutz's to be fully charged and enlarged.

WAY# (3.) <u>WORKING LATE</u>

Well you're probably way ahead of me on this one but let me say this about cheating men. Like water, they will take the path of least resistance. And how much resistance would you get about someone having to work late. This is his means of earning a living and certainly ranks high on the barometer of things to do in life. So there's little rebuttal from the woman other than what time will you be home? Yeah he's working late all right but whom is he working on? Any cheater will tell you the most intense and addictive type of sex you can get is from the workplace. Get in, get out, and get home! Let's give this a little more attention. Being confined to a certain area at a certain time with certain members of the opposite sex at some point will lead to sexual expectations. This is natural. It is in this type of arena where the most dedicated man can ultimately fall victim to their sexual subconscious.

WAY#(4.) <u>Send Flowers Anonymously To His Job</u>

Call this entrapment, low down, or down right unchristian. But if you choose to do so one of two things should happen.

A.) He comes home and tells you thank you for sending him flowers. This is a response of a man with nothing to hide and presumes that his lady must have sent them. Hint (GOOD.)

B.) He comes home and says nothing about receiving flowers at work. This is surely a sign this man has something to hide. It would imply that he has come on to so many women that he can't be sure whom the flowers are from and chooses to be silent and thought to be a fool, rather than to speak and remove all doubt. A medieval ass kicking would be in order for this man. Hint (VERY BAD.)

(Cheating men are like ice cream........Sweet, smooth and they usually head right to ALL <u>four</u> of your "(<u>LIPS</u>)", top & bottom!

WAY# (5.) <u>He Does Not Answer</u> <u>The Phone While You're Over</u>

If you and your man live in different places, and while visiting him he allows the answering service to pick up his calls while saying something like it's probably my job or just one of my homeboys. You can pretty much bet the farm that he's cheating on you. Fact of the matter is he knows more than likely it's the last woman he had sex with and a conversation with her in your presence, however short it is would be very awkward to say the least.

WAY# (6.) <u>He Will Not Allow You</u> <u>To Answer His Phone</u>

As stated in Way# (5.) It's the obvious reason you're not allowed to answer his phone and a typical response from a cheating man would be I pay the phone bill here and no one calling here would be asking for you anyway. This is a man with something to hide. (Hint.) The other woman.

Men who deal with one woman at a time, won't mind if you answer their phone because they have nothing to hide from you.

Now, If you can answer his CELL phone, then there is no reason to read any further. You have a rare keeper, not a common "creeper". Take him home to momma, grandmamma, and church on Sundays and you will do just fine.

WAY# (7.) <u>Frequent Ringing Cell Phone</u>

Unless you're man is a doctor, lawyer, drug dealer, or something along these lines. More than likely the other person on the line is a female with sexual intentions. Progressively the later the call comes the higher the probability it is the other woman he's cheating with. If a man is married and cheating, a cell phone is a must just by virtue of convenience and secrecy. This is his hotline to love and he will use it every chance he gets to get what he wants. The more frequently a mans cell phone rings, the higher the probability it's the other woman he's cheating with calling. `

WAY# (8.) <u>Star 69 His Phone</u>

Sneaky, but this is a good one! You must do this just at the right time. Like when you know he's been home by himself for a long time and he was the last one to use the phone. One big disadvantage for cheating men is the continual need to communicate.

Nothing is faster and easier than a phone call. In order to keep everything in order he must make sure that he calls the other woman as frequently as possible to keep her interested in him. So chances are you will get the other woman although it may take a number of attempts. The best time to do this #WAY is on his payday Friday or Saturday nights. Hit star 67 first to block the number then hit star 69 and listen carefully. If you here a soft sensual voice of a woman then suspect the obvious.......... *(THE OTHER WOMAN.)*

WAY# (9.) <u>GET A COPY OF HIS PHONE BILL</u>

Yes, I know this is an invasion of privacy but now is not the time to have a conscious. You can go to church later and ask God to forgive you, if you find nothing. Or go to church later and tell God thank you for showing you what a lowlife man you have been involved with. Phone bills give very specific information such as dates, time, telephone numbers, the lengths of conversations and names. If your man is cheating then the other woman's phone number will be on his phone bill. You can easily spot a pattern of calls and verify who that person is. If you have been dating your man for any length of time you should know where he keeps his phone bills, and if you don't know find out. For those of you who think this is beneath you that's ok because it's better to feel guilty now and know, than to not feel guilty and always be suspecting.

WAY# (10.) <u>LOOK THRU HIS BATHROOM TRASH</u>

You're probably saying "Holy Mother of all creatures large and small"; this is where I draw the line. However, you need to look thru his trash to find out if he's Trash! I know this sounds unsanitary, but with caution this could reveal some pretty incriminating evidence. Such as lipstick stained tissue, women's hygiene products, condom wrappers, the other woman's hair and things of the sort. Any of the items not affiliated to you would be very incriminating and hard to explain... *And believe me he will try!*

<u>*ANNOUNCEMENT:*</u>

THIS IS YOUR CAPTAIN SPEAKING; AS YOU CAN SEE WERE HEADED FOR SOME PRETTY ROUGH SEA'S AND THE SKY IS GETTING DARKER AND THE WIND IS GETTING WINDY AND THE SEA GULLS CAN ONLY BE SEEN NOT HEARD.

NOW WOULD BE A GOOD TIME TO PUT ON YOUR LIFE JACKET OF TRUTH!

I TOLD YOU BEFORE, ONCE YOU EMBARK ON THIS JOURNEY OF TRUTH THERE IS NO TURNING BACK. HOWEVER I HAVE MADE A EMERGENCY CONTINGENCY PLAN FOR THE WEAK & MEEK WHO WANT TO RETURN TO DENIAL LAND. WHAT THIS MEANS IS IF YOUR CONSCIOUS HAS CAUGHT UP WITH YOU JUST PUT THE DAMN MANIFESTO DOWN NOW! AND CONTINUE TO LIVE IN YOUR SHELL OF DOUBT AND INSECURITIES. DUMB DOESN'T HAVE A EXPIRATION DATE. FOR THE REST OF YOU PUT A CAPITAL "H" ON YOUR CHEST AND HANDLE THE "DAMN THING!"

@ NOW LET'S TAKE A MOMENT OF SILENCE FOR THE WEAK & MEEK!.............OK, THAT'S LONG ENOUGH.

AND FOR THOSE OF YOU WHO CONTINUE ON THIS CRUISE SHIP OF TRUTH, I COMMEND YOU.

I KNOW I SOUND INSENSATIVE AND RUDE, HOWEVER VERBAL SHOCK TREATMENT MAY BE NEEDED TO RESURRECT YOUR LIFE INTO EMOTIONAL ORDER! YOU CAN EITHER AGREE WITH ME OR BE WRONG! NOW IF THE INSULTS DON'T WORK LET'S SKIP THEM AND GET RIGHT TO YOUR ASS WHIPPING! (NOT REALLY.) THE TRUTH OFTEN DOES HURT BUT DENIAL CAN KILL YOU. SOME OF YOU WILL FEEL SO MISERABLE AFTER LEAVING YOUR MAN IT WILL FEEL LIKE YOU'RE STILL TOGETHER. (THINK ABOUT IT!).

CHEATING MEN ARE LIKE HARSH COLON CLEANSERS...THEY IRRITATE THE SHIT OUT OF YOU.

WAY# (11.) <u>Look For Strands Of Hair On His Pillows</u>

This alone isn't conclusive but certainly an indicator, particularly if the strands of hair that you find are not a match to anyone in the household. Another good place to look would be in his bathroom sink and around the bathroom floor. If indeed he has had female company she will certainly at some point go to the bathroom and comb her hair. Every woman sheds hair even if it's a wig. You should also check his passenger car seat for hair. Admittedly it takes a trained eye for this but if you focus this type of evidence can be found quite easily. Now if you find horse hair and your man does not belong to a rodeo then the other woman is either wearing a "cheap ass weave" or he's into horses: (literally.) This should only be considered circumstantial evidence but nonetheless, it is evidence.

WAY# (12.) <u>Abrupt Changes In Physical Appearance</u>

This is probably more noticeable among married men. When your man all of a sudden starts taking notice in his physical appearance by way of doing sit ups, push-ups, lifting weights, running, and so forth. This should be a concern. Ok! I hear what you're thinking, but please keep this in perspective with the rest of the listed #WAY'S. Because exercising alone would be a weak case. Every man that I interviewed agreed that just prior to cheating they were very concerned with their physical appearance. This also includes hygiene and dress.

WAY# (13.) <u>Being Stood Up</u>

For those of you who can relate to this one I feel most sorry for. Because this can only mean one thing: You are the other woman. Contrary to what he has made you believe by telling you that you are the only one.

Standing you up is nothing any man does purposely however when you're a cheating man, conflicts of schedules will happen. The fact is something more interesting came up in the form of a woman and persuaded him to change his plans.
Of course the next day he is very apologetic and starts to explain away his inconsiderateness because he feels guilty. The man's point of view on this is that they feel confident they won't lose you because of the great sex they give you when your together. Sounds vain but true. LADIES, to those of you out there who allow your man to stand you up I truly want to understand your point of view. But I can't quite seem to stick my head that far up my ASS!

WAY# (14.) <u>Verbal Attacks On You Over Something That's Not True</u>

As crude as this sounds, it is a reason for him to cheat on you without feeling guilty about it. The more conscientious a man is the more apt he is to use this technique. Because he needs a reason to be unfaithful to you and deep down he knows what he is saying is untrue. However this keeps you on the defensive the way he wants you to be. And this allows him to have justification for cheating on you. MY, MY, what a tangled web cheating men weave, when they deceive.

WAY# (15.) <u>Not Being Invited To Social Functions</u>

When comments are made like it's just going to be a bunch of men, the person who invited me did not say I could bring a guest, a friend gave me a ticket for only one, I know you don't like sports, and so forth, believe me when I say this........the old saying don't bring sand to the beach will more than lightly apply. He does not want to invite you because he knows that single women are going to be there. And it's a golden opportunity for him to go prospecting for more women. Now you should Invite Him, to kiss your ASS!

WAY# (16.) <u>Getting Flowers For No Apparent Reason</u>

This may be a tough one for you ladies to understand because most women love flowers. Which are symbolic to beauty and romance and give a euphoric feeling for that moment. It's no secret to men of the power of roses over women. So after cheating on you this is a cheap and effective way to wipe the slate clean in a cheating man's mind. That's right, he can insult you, mistreat you, beat you, not call you, stand you, cheat on you and so forth. Roses are like a free get out of jail card that works every time! If it's not your birthday, Valentine's Day, anniversary etc. etc., it is just his way of saying the unspoken; "I've been cheating on you with your best friend and I'm sorry". This most frequently happens among married couples and couples who live together.

Roses are red, violets are blue, and men who cheat, often give them to you.

WAY# (17.) <u>Physically Abusive Men</u>

As your Captain of truth, I would personally like to issue a behind the barn "Country Ass Whipping" to these type of men. However, due to such a large volume of them, time will not permit. If you are being physically abused by someone you love or think you need, take out a loan and buy yourself a clue! Or better yet, put the damn Manifesto down and go get help! I will all but guarantee you if he has no respect for your body he certainly will have no respect for his own body. Making him a high probability he will cheat on you. This is truly an untold story on planet Earth. I don't care what country, state or continent, there are millions of women who are physically abused by their men everyday. For those of you who are victims of this and continue to be victims of this please take a moment and look down at your shoes. Because you must of stepped in a great big pile of "Dumb Shit"!

REMEMBER: Men do to you what you let them do to you! (End of story.) So build a bridge and get over them!!!

WAY# (18.) <u>If You Met Him In A Nightclub</u>

This should not be a news bulletin. Men who frequent nightclubs and bars are promiscuous by virtue of just being there. You take a man married or not and put him in an environment of alcohol and dancing women and it's on and Crack'en. Chances are if you met him in a nightclub, he'll always be in a nightclub doing the same thing when he met you. Nightclubs are nothing more than an adult playground for cheater's who go there knowing that the probability of getting laid is only second to going to a Whore House. Cheaters will probably say I'm going out to have drinks with my buddies but in reality they're going out to shop for new women.

WAY# (19.) <u>If He Is Flirtatious</u>

I'm sure you're familiar with this type of man. He cannot resist the temptation to look and stare at other women. Even while in your company. Now don't get me wrong here, all men will notice woman just as much as they would a man, kids, car, dog, or anything else. But as faith will have it, the one day you get your man to go shopping with you it will seem as thou every HO! with a short skirt on within a radius of 50 miles will make it a point to cross paths with you and your man. And as the 2 of you try to act like you don't notice these fine young tender with long legs, bulging breasts, with "ASS'ES" you could set a drink on. The cheating man will give in to his Ho like tendencies even while your standing right next to him.

Once eye contact is mutual with the other woman, he will say hello or just make innocent unsuspecting conversation to the other woman. This type of man needs constant validation of his manhood and will engage women in conversation in any way he can. The more women that he can make notice him even in your presence, the more sexually confident he feels. Of course he will make derogatory comments to you about the women he has starred at or spoken to, after the fact. To keep you off guard such as how fat they are, look at what she's wearing, how their hair looks or anything to justify looking at other women. The same women he's slandering will be the same women he would try to get their phone numbers from. If these are the actions of your man while he's with you, what do you think his actions would be when he's alone? A man's eyes will tell it all if he is lusting after women. There are exceptions to this rule. If your man is cross-eyed or blind. When your man respects you he will maintain attention and

eye contact only to you.

WAY# (20.) <u>Will Not Show Affection For You Among Friends Or In Public</u>

Holding hands, a hug, a kiss, or walking with his arms around you just doesn't come natural for him. **HELLO!** Pull the blinders off your face and see him for what he does, not what he says. Believe me if he's not doing these things with you then he's doing these things with someone else. You probably try to justify his actions with the assumption he is shy or just inhibited romantically, when it's his cheating that should be prohibited.

If this is what you believe then let me pause for a moment and put my glasses on because; *<u>"I SEE DUMB PEOPLE!"</u>*

When a man love's you and is committed to you he will let you know, as well as anyone else how he feels about you. Showing open affection towards you in front of anyone is a man's way of marking his territory with hugs and kisses particularly if other men are present.

Now let's admit, this is far better than being urinated on.

WAY# (21.) <u>If He Is A Good Looking Man</u>

Well this goes without saying. Women are naturally attracted to handsome men and can be manipulated easier by them and they know it. Now let's do the math here. The better looking the man is the more women will be attracted to him. Raising the probability of him cheating on you. Most women will do just about anything to have a good-looking man by their side. And "HELL"! If he's that damn good looking then now you should ask the question; is he cheating with another man??? That's another book.

WAY# (22.) <u>He Did Not Want To Use A Condom The First Time You Had Sex</u>

This says a lot about your man and none of it is any damn good. Not only does he not care about your life, he doesn't care about his own.

To say the least, this man has low self-esteem. Which heightens the probability he is promiscuous. In other words, he's more concerned about the act of sex than the consequences it may bring. Indicating that he really doesn't care about you. This is the difference from having sex and making love....... In making love the man will show compassion for your well-being and feelings. If he was willing to roll the dice with you then he's certainly played this game before and will play it again and again. If a man doesn't care about himself, then how can he care for you? Certainly not wanting to wear a condom the first time you had sex would indicate this.

WAY# (23.) Men With Big Egos

This type of man always needs validation of their Manhood. The more women the better. Big egos need to be feed often and what could be a better source of food than a woman's affections. Seemingly this type of man has a way of separating morals from what he knows to be wrong.

His continual need to be the best and the center of attention makes him want to show off to any woman that will be his audience. This makes him at a higher risk for cheating on you.

WAY# (24.) <u>A Man Who Loses His Temper With You In The Presence Of Your Family Or Friends</u>

OK, you ask what does this have to do with cheating? Let me tell you.

It's all about **<u>"RESPECT!"</u>** If he shows no control over his temper in front of your family or friends, He will certainly have no control over his sexual desires.
Bad tempers usually indicate lack of self-respect and control. This man will react to emotions rather than common sense. This makes him more susceptible to cheating on you. For this type of man its lead me not to temptation, because he can find it all by himself. *(Cheating Men are like Earth Quakes......nothing can be done to STOP them.)*

WAY# (25.) <u>Men Who Won't Listen To You</u>

Ladies this is a simple one. When men don't listen to what you're saying it's because they don't care what you're saying.

All they know is when your mouth stops moving; THANK GOD! Now let's be more progressive here. If he doesn't care about what you're saying then he probably doesn't care about what you're feeling. And if he doesn't care about what you're feeling then he probably doesn't care about cheating on you because he doesn't care about being caught. When a man truly loves you he will listen to you completely and then respond with what he thinks is best for you. Looking you straight in your eyes while listening and responding. (Footnote): Sometimes I wonder? If a man was to speak in the woods, and there is no woman around to hear him, is he still wrong? (Answer): Only if he is a Cheating Man.

WAY# (26.) <u>When You're Man Makes The Statement: I Need Some Space</u>

Then show him how much space he has in his "Ass Hole" after you put your foot in it sideways with a twist! What he is really saying here is that I need some time to start a new relationship, or at least see what else is out there better than you. He will try and justify this with I need time to spend with my friends, family, job, studying, meditating and so on but don't believe the hype. If he has made this statement to you then your days of being together are numbered. Cut your losses and file for relationship bankruptcy now!

This is a relationship with only one end, and it's DEAD! As in dead end. These type men already have space, it can be found in their hollow head! Or I probably should say heads: (BIG & small) if you know what I mean.

WAY# (27.) <u>While Riding In The Car With Him He Stares At Other Women</u>

Relationships are all about making you feel like you are the only one. If while in your presence your man is eyeballing everything in a skirt, then what do you think he would be doing by himself in the car? THINKING OF HOW MUCH HE LOVES ONLY YOU! HELLO! HELLO! Did that Wizard ever get back to you about that brain??? Let me tell you what he's doing. Not only starring, probably honking the horn and ogling out of the window at them. All you need to do here is act like you're not looking at him while you are in the car with him and watch his eyes. Looking is one thing but glaring is another. And if you were to ask him what is he looking at? You would soon find that he suffers with C.R.S. (Can't Remember Shit.) Wondering eyes suggest a wondering heart. Wondering eyes that stare at other women are the sound tract to a cheating penis. Given the chance, the penis will dance.

Of course the cheating man will be in denial of any wrong doing however male cheaters can no more control staring at other women than they can control their penis. It's almost like a natural reflex for them to look and glare at other women so it will be easy to catch them in the act. Now how do you think he would feel and act if the situation where reversed? The answer is easy. Jealous first, then angry with their big egos hurt. Unfortunately cheating men are too busy thinking of themselves to even consider or notice you glaring at other men.

WAY# (28.) Meticulous Dresser

If you don't know this type of man you have certainly seen them. Wearing designer clothes with no wrinkles, shoes shined, color coordinated, nice jewelry, with hair and nails done. He knows exactly what he's wearing days before. This is an indicator that he wants to be noticed and not by the same-sex. (Hopefully!) This type of man is a walking billboard for attention and affection, with infection soon to follow. In other words, don't even act like you don't see me because I know I look DAMN-GOOD! At a minimum. Women are going to notice this man even if he isn't good-looking. Contrary to what you might believe. Nice clothes can make a man more appealing giving him more advantage if he chooses to cheat. Now, if he's a good-looking man and a meticulous dresser the question is not if he will cheat on you but when and how often? Of course there are exceptions to this logic...... If he's the minister of a Church. Hmmm, I could be wrong on this one.

WAY# (29.) <u>A Man Who Shows No Respect For His Mother</u>

If this fits your man's M.O. then run don't walk away from this man. You're on a dead-end street with no lights at the end of the tunnel. If a man can't honor the most important woman in his life then what is there to be said for you? I'm sure not much. He doesn't acknowledge his mother on Mother's Day, Christmas, her Birthday, and so forth. He swears in front of her and sometimes to her. He has no respect for her words or wisdom, then be warned.

His mother may have told him: "Son you can be anything you want to be"! But I'm sure an ass-hole was not one of them.

A man who does not honor his mother won't hesitate not to honor you. Making more likely the chance he will cheat on you every change he gets.

Drop this man like the bad habit he is. But before you do, open up a can of Whip Ass and **KICK HIS ASS FOR ME!!!**

WAY# (30.) <u>A Man With No Religious Background</u>

A man without religion is a lost soul. Like a left handed man who always thinks he's right. The essence of who we are and what we believe in must be nourished by the word of God. Without His divine guidance, bad decisions will be made time and time again. The ability to choose between right and wrong becomes cloudy and dark. So when confronted with a situation to cheat or not to cheat It will be easier to go the way of the flesh. This type of man may not have it together, but together with God, he can have it all. If you want a rainbow you have to put up with the rain. That means with the right spiritual training he can change his cheating ways.

WAY# (31.) <u>He's Not A Gentleman</u>

He doesn't open your car door, he doesn't help you to be seated, he is un-polite, he swears in front of you, doesn't help you when you need help.

This just simply means he doesn't care about your well being or he is just too ignorant to know the difference between what's right and wrong. Either way, these are indicators of low self-esteem and selfishness. Which you should know by now means a higher probability he will be promiscuous. And if he's not a gentleman by now chances are he will never be one.

WAY# (32.) <u>The Alcoholic</u>

Drinking alcohol is an excuse to be someone else that normally HE would not be. Angry, funny, not shy, bold, daring, stupid, silly, happy, and the list goes on and on. Rated very high on this list is sexuality because of the effects of alcohol in lowering one's inhibitions and ability to make rash sensible decisions. Such as to cheat on my wife or not to cheat on my wife? To be confronted with a situation where this decision needs to be made, the more drinks he has the more likely he will cheat if confronted with that situation.

When drinking most men like to play carpenter! First they get hammered. Then they want to nail you. After all there is always the excuse I was drunk and don't remember. Cheating men call this (D.S.A.) Drunk Selective Amnesia. Drinking and making bad decisions go together like RUM and Coke or a Nunn and a Pope.

WAY# (33.) Leave One Of Your Earrings On His Car Seat

With this one I hope that he tells you he found your earring on his car seat in a reasonable amount of time. If not, one of two things has occurred. (A.) He found your earring and forgot to tell you. (B.) He found your earring and was not sure whose earring it could belong to because he's had so many women in his car. So he holds on to it and waits for someone to ask for it. If it's the latter, then chances are he is cheating on you. If you're not sure it's (A.) OR (B.), then more testing needs to be done. Reference WAY# (34.)

WAY# (34.) Leave A Pair Of Your Underwear In His Bedroom

The key here is to leave a pair of your underwear in a place in the bedroom that you know he will find them. like at the foot of the bed. Now when he finds them he should just put them aside and let you know you forgot something next time he

talks to you.

If still no response refer to WAY # (35.).

WAY# (35.) <u>Ask Your Man Leading Questions</u>

For example: Tell him you are missing some personal items and ask if he has found them. A man with something to hide would probably ask you what items are you missing? Only because he wants to be sure that the items he has belongs to you. Now when he shows you the item or items act surprised like they don't belong to you and ask whom do they belong to? Now observe his reaction. If he starts to act asinine, dense, dull, dumb, slow, unintelligent and says that they must belong to his sister, mother, niece, cousin, maid, or Mother Teresa, know that this is a typical response from a cheating man. If you're the only woman he is seeing then he should respond to you with the confidence that they could only belong to you. If you are still not sure in determining guilt or innocence then pay close attention to WAY# (36.).

WAY# (36.) <u>Set Up A Sting Operation</u>

This involves the use of one of your girlfriends or job associates that he doesn't know. Have her call him at his job while you listen in on a three-way conversation. Have her pretend she's a secret admirer and wants to know if he's available to meet for dinner. Her treat. If he is the HO! That you suspect him to be he will agree to meet her for dinner. But you show up instead! Be prepared to catch his face because I know it will break when he sees you instead. Talk about food for thought. (No pun Intended.) This will make for a very interesting conversation over dinner. Somehow, I think he will lose his appetite. Oh by the way make sure he pays for the dinner. If there is any player in your man he will fall for this hook line and sinker. If he doesn't take the bait I think you have a keeper. If he does go for it cut your losses and get out of the relationship because it's his nature to a cheater for life.

WAY# (37.) <u>The Use Of Time Related Items In This Sting Operation</u>

Plant a lipstick stain on a glass in his kitchen. By using this method now you have the advantage in that it can't be explained away by saying oh, my last girlfriend must of left that. The evidence of lipstick on the glass indicates a certain time frame. Mainly recently, and would need a more specific explanation. Same effectiveness with lipstick stained cigarettes, sanitary napkins in trash, and hair in the bathroom sink that's a different type from your own. I think you get the idea. Now ask him about what you found? An innocent response would be I don't know, it has to be yours. If indeed he has been cheating the evidence is so compelling that he will have to tell you something even if it's not the truth. Although you planted the evidence the nature of his ambiguous explanation would imply he has been cheating on you!

WAY# (38.) <u>He Keeps An Extra Change Of Clothes In The Trunk Of His Car</u>

The thought process of a cheating man is to leave home in unassuming clothes that will not bring any attention to his intention to see another woman. And in "her trunk" is junk in the shape of 2 basketballs (ass). Then he goes over his buddy's house to change clothes. As out of the way as this may sound I have had many married men tell me that this is what they do so as to not bring any suspicion while pursuing other women. The lady of the house would be very unsuspecting to see her man leave the house in shorts and a dirty tee shirt as oppose to suited and booted. So check the trunk of your mans car for this type of evidence.

WAY# (39.) <u>Check For Extra Used Towels In His Bathroom</u>

This would be mainly for washcloths. However, bath towels as well. If your relationship has been for any meaningful length of time then this information you should know. Where the towels are kept and how many he has clean. You should also be aware of how he keeps his towels hanging, number of towels, and the position of the towels. You should also check is dirty clothes hamper in case he has the presence of mind to put used towels away. I never said this would be easy or sanitary, but you must do what you have to do to find out if your man is cheating. With that being said examine the towels for physical evidence such as hair, odor, or bodily fluids. If your man has been cheating than certainly the other woman has used towels to clean up leaving physical evidence behind. Most guys on an average will use a wash @ dry towel for at least a week or more. Gross but true. This little statistic will make it very easy to determine when towels are unaccounted for. The idea here is just to gather more pieces of the puzzle to be assembled at a later date. NOTE: the dirty towels may be

tested for his semen. Refer to Way #(92.).
Offer to wash his clothes and
you can easily find and remove evidence.

WAY# (40.) <u>Check His Video Or DVD Player</u>

Chances are you will learn valuable information here such as the porno movie he was last watching without you being there. This brings a lot of questions to mind as to with whom and why he is watching porno, especially without you. The implication here is that he is having a secret sex life that does not include you. It is only logical to assume that there is some part of his sexuality that he does not want you to know about. (Probably a chronic masturbator!) What ever the case may be it is still a form of cheating and if he is hiding this from you then what else related to sex is he hiding. Look thru the rest of his video collection and be prepared for what you will find. The more sex tapes you find the more likely this man will cheat on you. Cheating always starts in the mind first, and if he's watching porno with out you then phase one (The mind) is in effect with the body (Penis) soon to follow.

WAY# (41.) ODORS!

This potentially could be one of your best clues. By way of odors, I mean female related odors that don't belong to you. Such as pussy, perfumes, lotions, cologne, body spray fragrances, and things of the sort that could linger for days. If you detect anything that's suspect then next smell the middle finger of your man's right hand. (Left hand if he is left-handed.) Do this in a way that is very unsuspecting by holding his hand and at some point kiss the hand and smell the middle finger. If you smell an odor other than your own it's obvious that he's been picking more than just his nose. A woman's love juice on a man's finger cannot be washed off very easily. It needs to wear off. Also check his crotch, couch, pillows, bed, and towels for any other female odors. If your man has a mustache or beard also check there for any smells of snapper and I don't mean red snapper. Every time a man cheats there will always be evidence to find if you know how to look for it.

WAY# (42.) Look Through His Photo Albums

All players keep photos of their female conquests. I call them visual trophies. This will require getting a little nosy around his home. If he has not already shown you his photo album it's probably for a reason. There is something or someone he does not want you to see. And even if he has shown you his photo album all players keep an X-rated photo album of their woman past and present. Now I must warn you to be mentally prepared for what you might see. Yes, that calm care free easy going nice guy that you thought was only committed to you could be the "freak of all freaks"! Getting laid as often as possible. Seek and ye shall find, find and ye shall see!

WAY# (43.) Check Through His Clothing Pockets

Go through all his shirt, coat, and pants pockets. I will guarantee you; you'll find many items of special interest.

The most compelling items you'll find are phone numbers of women. Even a want to be player will test his skills every now and then to see how many phone numbers he can collect. It's kind of a confirmation of a man's manhood. Among some of the items you will find will be old theater tickets, parking validation tickets, restaurants receipts, concert tickets, motel receipts and so forth which will all reveal specific information such as dates and times when you know it was not you that was with him. Can you spell *BUSTED!*
Because this is what he will surely be.

WAY# (44.) A Very Spoiled Man

Adult men who as a child were use to getting their way, particularly by their mothers have the same expectations as men. But now other "women" have replaced the image of the mother. That is to say if he feels there's something that one woman won't do, He will seek the attention from another woman to fill that void. As the term "SPOILED" implies; rotten, not good, sour, gone bad, so will this type of man when he is in a relationship. Making him more likely a candidate to cheat on you.

WAY# (45.) <u>Men Who Constantly Forget Birthdays And Anniversaries</u>

Well you say what man has not been guilty of this. The key point here is constantly. We all make mistakes. But for those men who genuinely care and love you and are devoted only to you will remember these special days with love, gifts, and lots of attention. For a cheater you will find that he suffers with C.C.R.S. *(Chronically Can't REMEMBER SHIT!)* He considers these special days as just another way to extort money from him. And when you have more than one woman you can see why they really don't forget. They just don't want to remember for costs reasons $$$.

FOOD FOR THOUGHT: MEN ARE LIKE PARKING SPACES.........ALL THE GOOD ONES ARE ALWAYS TAKEN, THE REST ARE HANDICAPPED!

WAY# (46.) <u>Men With Ex-girlfriends Whom They Claim Are Just Friends</u>

By the POWER of "CHRIST" I compel thee, By the POWER of "CHRIST" I COMPEL THEE! Ladies, use you're commonsense here. This is a person or persons whom he knows intimately. And I used the word intimately to refer to more than just in a sexual manner. He knows her favorite color, the food she likes, the music she listens to, the amount income she earns, her favorite flowers, perfume, how she walks, how she thinks and on and on and on. Excuse my language here, but this is like having a savings account of pussy! When he wants to he can withdraw as much out as he likes with no penis penalty for early withdrawal. As a matter of fact as much as 80% of the time when a man cheats it's with an ex-girlfriend. Remember as stated before. Sexually, men will travel the path of least resistance like free-flowing water. It's easier for a man to get sex from someone he is already had sex with them from someone he doesn't know at all.

WAY# (47.) <u>Woman's Intuition</u>

Call it a sixth sense if you will, but to put it clear and simple if you feel your man is cheating on you, then he probably is. This is different from thinking your man is cheating on you. To think your man is cheating is just admitting that there is a possibility for this to happen. However to feel your Man is cheating is the collective evaluation and observations of what you know he's really like. There's also the spiritual aspect to this feeling, which I will try to explain. Men who cheat give energy which causes a depletion in their spiritual aura and at the same time they are receiving spiritual energy from the other woman. Which is something different from his own energy or aura. Consequently when he returns in your presence this is what you're sensing in your subconscious mind. Like electricity you can't see it but you feel it and know it's there. The other woman's energy that he brings home to you will linger for days. And like electricity will shock you into knowing the Truth!

WAY# (48.) <u>The Bluff!</u>

Bluffing is a technique using certain known facts about your man along with what you think you know about your man to intimidate him into telling the "TRUTH". Timing, diplomacy and a true look of sincerity must be co-mingled together in order to get this to be effective. You set the stage by announcing you have something very serious you would like to talk to him about regarding your relationship with him. Now here's where the bluff begins. Tell him you have found out some very specific information and need him to be honest now and you will forgive him. At this point in his mind is in a whirlpool of thoughts wondering what in the HELL! you have found out. Now he is definitely on the defensive if he has something to hide. Under this circumstance cheating men have a talent for making the smallest amount of lying go the furthest way so beware. A man with a clear conscious would be on the offensive not defensive. Demanding to know what is it that you think you know? Asking what possibly could be the problem while maintaining good eye contact with you all the time. A cheaters reaction to the bluff will at first be total silence because he is thinking of a ton of excuses and lies. Watch his face carefully and note if his eyes are moving side to side and if he does not maintain go eye contact with you. This is an indicator he is using parts of his brain he didn't even know he had.

CAPTAIN'S MEMO; IF THE LEFT SIDE OF YOUR BRAIN CONTROLS THE RIGHT SIDE OF YOUR BODY; DOES THIS MEAN ONLY LEFT HANDED PEOPLE ARE IN THEIR RIGHT MIND?

Now in a calm direct voice ask him point blank. "Are you Cheating on Me?" NOW STOP, LOOK AND LISTEN. Observe facial expressions, eye contact and body movement or bowel movement at this point. If you get a nod of the head, a shrug of the shoulders, hand gestures, shuttering, sneering facial expressions and no eye contact would be indicative of guilt.

Keep your questions short, clear, easily

understood and confined to the topic. Any attempt to evade answers, change the subject, give vague answers, or inconsistent answers along with nervousness are signs of lies. Remember keep the illusion that you have information that you know he is cheating on you. This technique is more effective than you will ever realize.

CAPTAIN'S MEMO; MEN ARE LIKE STOCK BONDS............THEY TAKE SO LONG TO MATURE..........(SEXUALLY)!

WAY# (49.) Stops Being Available

At first you won't even notice it because he will be so smooth and believable with his excuses. But then you notice a pattern of behavior that is quite different than when the relationship was fresh and new. Ladies! I know the truth can hurt but the fact is he is not available because he has found someone new! This does not mean she is prettier than you or has a better figure than you. It's just the thrill of the "Hunt" or should I say "Cunt". A cheating man's instinct is to seek, meet and conqueror.

Weak excuse but true.

It's just the novelty that she's new and cheaters live for this challenge of a new conquest. Once he has succeeded then he will make himself more available to you again, and in time you will see the pattern start all over again. This is how cheating men navigate from woman to woman or more accurately how *"Players Play the Game"*.

Tighten up your seat belts for the next one. This will shock you!

Way# (50.) <u>Men Who Go To Church But Often By Themselves</u>

The church is the new modern-day nightclub or should I say day club? How many other places can you think of with so many beautiful well-dressed women with a glow of innocence? These women are particularly vulnerable to church going men. Now let's put this in perspective. Men don't have to pay for parking, admission into the church, does not have to pay for drinks or dinner, no purchase of roses, and it's optional to give a donation. (sometimes)

For virtually no upfront money he can have his pick of beautiful unsuspecting women. Here you have the scenario of letting the wolf in the sheep's den under the disguise of a God fearing man. Under these circumstances the man has many advantages. (1.) He can see very clearly. (2.) He's not drunk. (3.) Any woman he speaks to would be obligated by God to speak back. (4.) He only needs to learn one dance. *(THE HOLY GHOST)*.

Usually it's the more seasoned cheater who would employ this sly technique.

WAY# (51.) Unemployed Men

This circumstance could bring the player out of any man. This means that desperate times call for desperate measures. If a man can be successful in getting money out of one woman, then why not run the same game on another woman and another. Basically the more women he can get money from, the more comfortable he becomes with his situation. Unemployment becomes his reason for cheating.

A man with no job will have plenty of time for cheating while you are hard at work. An unemployed man can bring you down lower than a "Midget" on his knees!

CAPTAIN'S MEMO: *WHY ARE WISE MEN AND WISE ASSES TOTAL OPPOSITES?*

WAY# (52.) Men Who Watch Porno

To a cheater, porno is nothing more than visual foreplay. Have you ever heard of association a-simulation? By the virtue of what porno represents (promiscuity) it would be logical to assume he would have a certain curiosity of what it would be like to experience what he is viewing. After all most men feel watching porno is watching something that would never happen to them, however they will try to get you to do some of the things they have watched. And for all the things you ladies say you would never do such as anal sex, orgies, oral sex, mate swapping and so forth. Well guess what? He will find someone who will. For this type man his brain should be frozen

until they find a cure some day for this sexual addiction.

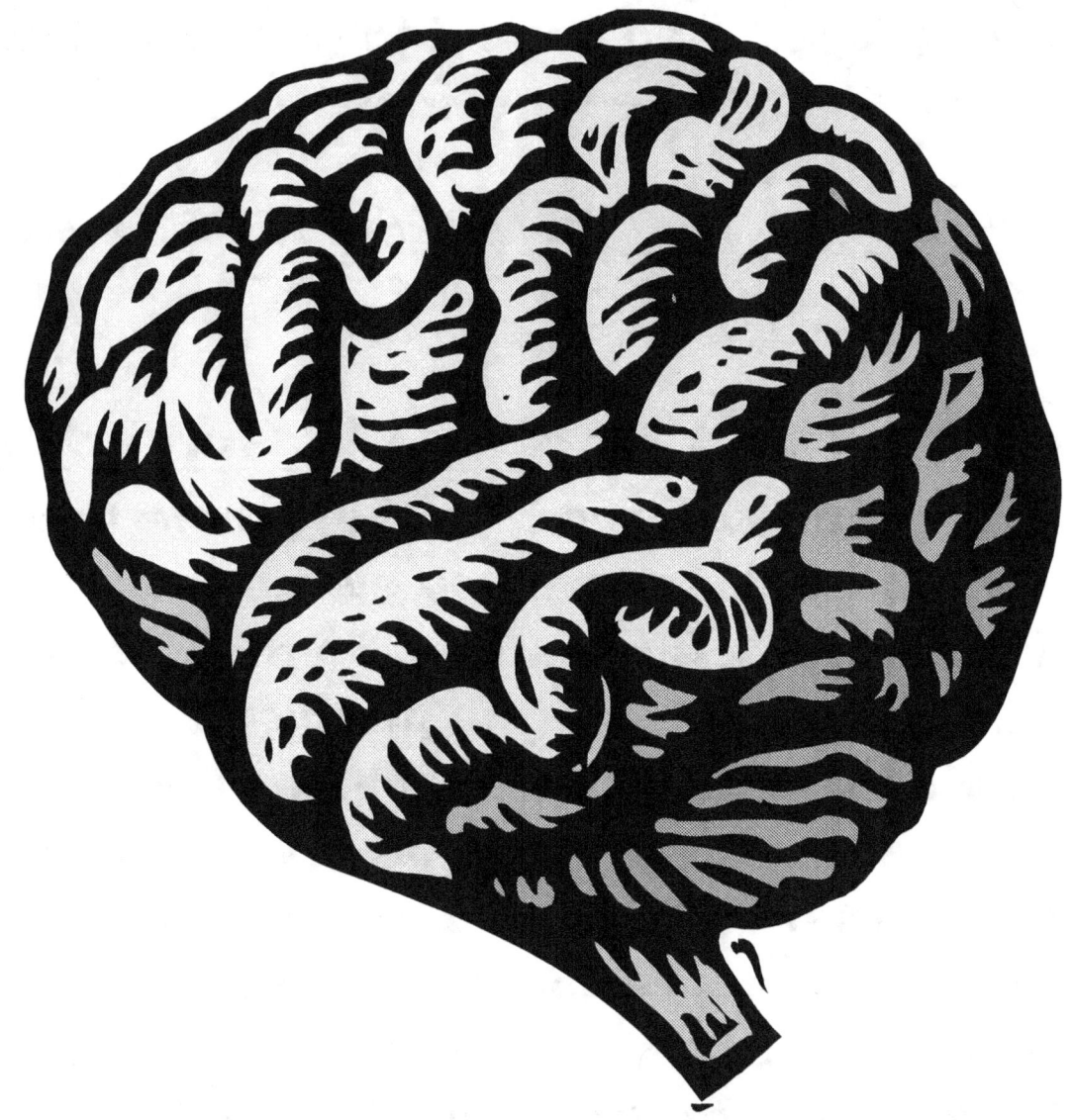

Well don't get your hopes up here for a future cure! Cheating men are stuck on stupid.

A man watching young naked women will surely lust for them. This alone is a form of Cheating mentally.

WAY# (53.) <u>Frequent Vaginal Infections</u>

Most men don't understand how easy it is to transfer bacteria and viruses from woman to woman. They are under the illusion that hot water and soap will clean them and prevent infections from happening. This could not be further from the truth. In the defense of the men, unfortunately there are often no symptoms of their infections. So he is clueless of the infections he spreads. When you hear the term sexually transmitted diseases (STD's) most men will think of gonorrhea, syphilis, AIDS, chlamydia and genital herpes. The fact of the matter is that these are some of the identifiable few. There is currently an epidemic going on with sexually transmitted viruses for which there is no symptoms or cure for men.

I'm somewhat off the topic but due to the importance of this issue I will spend a little more time and try to keep it plain and truthful. It is my opinion that the average doctor is not informed enough about the latest sexually transmitted viruses that have little if any symptoms in a man. So even if the man is conscientious about his health and goes to the doctor for a checkup. Chances are, none of the testing will show anything wrong. So off he goes thinking he has a clean bill of health. The symptoms of genital viruses in a woman are a lot more severe causing Infertility, tumors, fibroids, bleeding, discharge, cancer, hysterectomies and severe stomach cramps. At last count there is an estimated 80 mutations of the herpes virus that is highly contagious infecting the membrane of the sex organs. The evidence if any in a man is a small cluster of bumps that can easily go undetected. It's estimated that 1 in 3 people are infected and the numbers are growing. The irony here is that most people are unaware of this threat. What is truly frightening about this strain of viruses know as HPV (Human Papilloma Virus) is that even if you use a condom the virus is so contagious and microscopically small that it can still be transferred from skin to skin contact. It can also survive in pubic hair giving a burning symptom like jock itch and under fingernails. For more scientific information go to your web browser and enter sexual viruses. Most women dismiss frequent infections as just yeast infections, which they considered to be normal. Vaginal odors are usually a result of a cheating penis! Well enough Shock and Awh.

WAY# (54.) Passion Marks

This one is somewhat self-explanatory, but does take a trained eye to spot it. Skin discoloration and bruises about the neck, scratch marks on the back and arms that you know you didn't put there would be a clue he's cheating or has been wrestling with a octopus or octo-pussy.

WAY# (55.) <u>Swollen Penis</u>

When any part of the human anatomy is overused or abused there are side effects. One of which is a swollen red penis when used to frequently. When men are sexually active with more than one woman and trying to satisfy them all is nothing more than penis abuse. The thousands of tiny blood vessels can become ruptured and constrict the blood from flowing freely back out of the penis giving it a balloon look in an unexcited state. To put this more simply, if your man's penis looks different than what you're used to seeing then red flags should go up. (Or should I say red penis). Touch and fondle his penis and watch if he shows signs of discomfort and pain, if so then the obvious would be true. He's been using his penis for more than just urination.

WAY# (56.) <u>Smell His Penis</u>

I can only imagine the look on your face

from the thought of this but grin and bear it, to "Smell", if he has been sharing it! As mentioned before men are under the impression that what ever will let them stick their penis into, that hot water and soap with maybe a little cologne will somehow make them clean and undetectable of any previous sexual activities. The fact of the matter is female secretions usually have to wear off. No matter how much he washes, the scent of the other woman will still be on his penis. Just like no two fingerprints are identical. There are no two vaginal scents that are the same. And being a woman, you will easily discern between penis odor and vaginal secretions. And like perfume if you know it's not your scent, then it makes no since to continue the cheating relationship.

WAY# (57.) <u>Men Who Rush Into Relationships</u>

The problem here is usually they leave the relationship just as quickly as they get into it. And when I say "GET INTO IT" I mean it

literally!
The faster he can con you into a so called
relationship to get what he wants, the
faster he wants out of the relationship.

A sure sign of this type of cheater is his
persistence to get you into bed the first
time you meet. He will say and do almost
anything if he feels it will get him what he
wants. He will win your affection to give
you a infection if you are not careful.

This type of man normally does not give total closer when leaving a relationship so quickly. So one relationship overlaps with another relationship and another. The result is sleeping with more than one woman at a time. The objective of this type a man is to give the illusion that he's looking for a long-term relationship. Making it easier for the woman to trust him and give in to his sexual desires. The faster he can gain your confidence In thinking you are the one and only, the faster he gets what he wants in the way of sex, money, or favors. This man is like *"Diarrhea" ;they shit fear at the first sign of commitment.*

WAY# (58.) <u>He Doesn't Keep His Word About Calling</u>

Plain and simple if someone tells you they are going to call you then this is exactly what you should expect. It is frustrating to be at home anticipating a promised call that doesn't happen. The more time that goes by, the more upset you become.
As a matter of fact, it brings out many

emotions of which none are any good. Anger, anxiety, anxiousness, fear of accidents, another woman or just a bad memory are all thoughts that one may have as a result of a broken promise to call. Usually when a man makes a promise about calling you it's because at the time they think this is what you want to hear and it's so easy to say. However out of sight out of mind as he continues down his list of possible female suitors. Not calling you is only an indication that you are not that important to him and even if he does remember he said he would call you he can't because he's in the company of another woman. *THINK ABOUT IT.*

WAY# (59.) <u>Men Who Drive Fast Sports Cars</u>

There seems to be a parallel here. Fast cars..... Fast men. This type of man likes female attention and his sports car is a way of getting it.

This is his way of saying to women hey look at me. I'm available. The car is a mirror reflection of his lifestyle *(fast)*, making him a more likely candidate for cheating in a relationship. The fact that his car does not have room for kids is a statement in itself. "I don't want a family and I want to be free of responsibility and commitment".

Captain's memo: In the above reference to kids, I don't quite understand the concept of training them.

You spend the first three years teaching them how to walk and talk and the next 15 years telling them to sit down and shut the"_ _ _ _ " up!

WAY# (60.) <u>Men Who Wear Turtlenecks</u>

This could potentially be a way to hide passion marks more commonly referred to as monkey bites about the next area. Simply check his neck for passion marks. Women are more into giving monkey bites then men.

It's an unspoken way of marking their territory and regardless of the pain; men will allow this to happen as a sign of their endurance and masculinity. It's always after the fact when the man looks into the mirror and then realizes how hard it would be to explain the bruises. An easier alternative would be to wear a turtleneck or a high button up collar shirt to cover it up.

WAY# (61.) <u>Keep Inventory Of His Condoms</u>

Here you only need to know simple math. If there were six condoms in bob's pack and bob used one on you, and the next time you see bob, there are only three condoms then what happened to number four and five? If you fall for the story he was practicing using them on a banana, I let my friend borrow some, I used them in a water balloon fight or two were defective. I will bitch slap you about the head and face until commonsense jumps into your ass! Well of course, I'm just kidding about the violence but as your Captain and Mentor sometimes shock value is the best therapy.

WAY# (62.) <u>If You Witness Your Man Lying To His Friends</u>

People lie mostly to avoid hurting others, to gain something or to stay out of trouble. If you hear your man lying about something to his friends then it is a safe assumption he will lie to you under similar conditions. You could argue that everyone lie's about something but the point to be made is the unnecessary lying were the truth would have served just as good. These are the type of men that if you tell them about something, the next person they tell the same story to will knowingly add things just for the sake of making it sound more interesting. If this is a trademark of your man then he is more lightly to say what sounds better as oppose to saying the truth to his friends. Most certainly he will do the same to you when it comes to cheating.

WAY# (63.) If You Witness Your Man Lying To A Family Member

If this be the case you're pretty much S.O.L. (SHIT OUT OF LUCK!) Without a doubt he has been lying to you as well. Things like where he has been, what he has been doing, who he was with, where he is going, you're the only one for me, how much money he earns and so forth are subject to raised eyebrows. This is indicative of a man with low morals and ethics, pointing the finger (The Middle) towards someone who will cheat on you in a heartbeat.

Way# (64.) *This Is a Good One!* Go Downtown To The Hall Of Records And Check His Criminal Background

You would be amazed at the wealth of information you can find on a person by just knowing their name. So much information is public notice and may be

viewed by anyone who inquires.
Any arrests, felony convictions, divorces, property ownership, real birth dates, and much more. These days you never know much personal information about the person that you are involved with other than what they want you to know. That warm loving man you have given your heart and "HOLE" to, could be wanted for murder! You say invasion of privacy? I say persuasion of Truth. The information that you find out can help you judge this man's character and make a better decision about your love investment.

WAY# (65.) Men Who Are Available Only At Weird Hours

10pm,11pm and after mid-night. As the saying goes what you do in the dark will come to light! Take your blindfold off and see the situation for what it is. To put it plain and simple you are the booty call, getting leftovers. His primetime is being spent with the woman who he loves and values more than you.

I can hear what you're thinking, but the sex is so good. The truth is, what's good to you may not be good for you.

CAPTIAN'S ANNOUNCEMENT

Pussy makes promiscuous men lose their ability to interpret the future. This means seeking an immediate lesser reward over the greater reward with you in the future. This is often referred to as thinking with the "DICK" head instead of the Big head.

WAY# (66.) Men Who Cheat At Games

Basketball, chess, golf, tennis, cards, dominoes, checkers, monopoly, bingo, or just the game of life. If he'll cheat while playing a game, he will cheat on you just the same. A leopard can't change his spots, but a cheater can and will change the score of a game to his favor. A cheater is a cheater. And if you witness your man cheating at games beware of this man because he'll have no shame and will do you the same. Trying to win at getting other women's affections will be a game he will play often. Connect the dots and think outside the box for a moment. This man has no ethics with morals soon to follow as long as he wins!

WAY# (67.) <u>Men Who Call You Baby All The Time</u>

Or any other generic name he could say to any woman. In the numerous interviews I have done with men, I found it quite surprising almost all of them had a story to tell about calling their woman by someone else's name at some point in their relationships. Cheating men have learned through trial and error that is much safer just to call all their women by the name "Baby" or what ever other generic name he has chosen for you. Especially during Intimate moment's when the conscious mind becomes more subconscious. Calling you baby is like having a cheap insurance policy against certain liability if he were to call you by the wrong name especially during love making. Now when you hear him say ooh baby, ooh baby, yeah baby, yeah baby, cancel this cheap low budget, low down insurance policy by asking him, What's my name? What's my name?

WAY# (68.) Men Who Don't Answer Their Door

It's for all the obvious reasons. He knows it could be any number of the other women he is currently sleeping with. Observe him as he looks thru the peak-hole of his door and if he quietly walks away know that another woman is on the other side. And if he chooses not to answer the door at all, or even look it's because he's not sure who may be on the other side in the form of a woman. Of course your going to hear excuses for not answering the door like it's just the manager, that's my home-boy, I don't want to be bothered, it's just my neighbor, damn those Jehovah Witnesses, it's the Avon lady, and if they didn't call first, then they're not Invited. The fact is, they have been calling but he doesn't answer his phone or return their phone calls because he's busy with you. So they decided to just stop by unannounced and as faith will have it, it will be at the most inconvenient time like when your there.

****** **READER ALERT!** ******

Once again as a reminder for the most part it is usually a combination of #WAY'S that indicates your man is cheating. Individually the #WAY'S don't give cause for great alarm but rather a greater awareness of what could be.

WAY# (69.) *As The Number Symbolizes (69):* Men Who Won't Eat The Coochie

Men who will not go down on a woman don't have enough appreciation and respect for God's gift to man. Cheaters have so many women that they feel no obligation to give oral sex. The other men who are not so lucky would praise your body head to toe and would consider it a privilege to give you oral pleasure because they want to be committed only to you. As the saying goes you need to lick it before you stick It. Show me a woman whose man does not perform oral sex on her and I will show you a woman who is sexually frustrated.

I don't care how good the conventional sex is, if he does not go down, then he should not be around! It's like having cookies with no milk, grits without the butter, or a car without gas. As long as the streets are clean there should be no problem taking a walk down them. A man who does not have oral sex with his woman is like driving his car without insurance. If another man does what he won't do then he will have to assume all liability.

WAY# (70.) Call Your Man Late At Night When You Know He Should Be Home

If he does not answer the phone, leave a message in a normal manner. Then do a drive-by. NO! NO! Not south central style but drive past his home and look for signs if he's there. Like his car in the driveway or an unfamiliar car in the driveway, lights on in the house, the silhouette of someone through the window. Or get out of the car and listen for sounds of music or voices.

Also smell, for any women's perfumes that may linger around his front door. In so many cases I have found that cheating men will call and talk to their girlfriends at night to give them the illusion that they are tired from work and will be soon going to bed when they finish their conversation with you. The truth is when the cat's away the mice will play. This means they have made plans for female company to come over once they have confirmed the coast is clear. The cheating man feels confident that there will be no interuption from his girlfriend because she thinks he's home tired and sleeping. He's sleeping all right but sleeping around would better discribe the situation. If you determine that he is at home then call again from a different number that he cannot identify and see if he answers the phone. If he still does not answer then more than lightly he has female company over and does not want to be bothered. If he does answer the phone make up a reason to stop by and listen to his response.

If he comes up with some reason or reasons why you cannot stop by, then more than likely the latter is true. He is up to no good and will give you plenty of attitude.

WAY# (71.) <u>Men Who Seem To Good To Be True</u>

This seems to happen to all women at least once. Your knight in shining armor who's going to whisk you off your feet and carry you off into the sunset with expectations of marriage, a house with a white picket fence, a sports utility vehicle, a dog with a kid on the way. Somehow in your mind you convince yourself that "GOD" has finally answered your prayers as you let everyone know about him. Yeah but the marriage soon turns to wreckage, the house is in foreclosure, the picket fence never got put up, your sports utility vehicle is a YUGO with a luggage rack, and the only dog you have is him, with a kid on the way soon to be on welfare. Ladies! The rule of thumb is if it sounds too good to be true then it isn't.

This is a sure sign of a veteran cheater. He simply presents himself in a way that sweeps you off your feet and onto your back. And if you think for one minute that somehow you are the only woman he has appealed to in this way then you must believe in that lucky rabbit's foot on your key-chain.

FOOD FOR THOUGHT: If a rabbit's foot is so lucky, _then what happened to the rabbit?_

WAY# (72.) <u>Ask To Switch Cell Phones For A Day</u>

Preferably on a Friday or Saturday. Out of all the #WAYS listed this may be the most difficult to employ. I would suggest that this #WAY be used only under the pretense that you feel very strongly that your man is cheating and you have confronted him about it and he strongly denies it. This would be an opportune time to ask him: If you love me like you say you do and have nothing to hide then let's switch cell phones for a day. (WARNING!) Now if you are cheating then forward all your calls to your mother's house before handing him your cell phone. Now take a step back and look, listen and observe. A cheating man's reaction would be raised eyebrows with a statement like; Bitch! You must be crazy. Of coarse he will only be thinking that part. This will surely be followed by excuses like I need my cell phone because the following people may call that I must talk to right then and there like>>>>>>>>>>>>>>>>

1.) HIS BOSS
2.) HIS MOTHER
3.) HIS KIDS
4.) HIS PAROLE OFFICER
5.) HIS BUDDIES
6.) HIS BOOKIE
7.) HIS PRIEST
8.) HIS UNCLE
9.) HIS X-WIFE
10.) HIS OTHER WOMAN***(BINGO!)

Your come back to this should be you will call him on your phone as soon as you receive any calls. Continue maintaining good eye contact with him as more signs of discomfort manifest themselves by way of stuttering, sweating, wondering eyes, pacing, and possible fainting. BEWARE! This will have the consequences of backing a wild starving mountain lion into a corner. With nowhere to go he will attack. Check his underwear later and you will see the only mark a cheating man will leave in life is in his underwear. Before this cheating man will give you his C_ell, he would rather go to H_ell.

WAY# (73.) When You Call Him Late-Night And His Line Is Always Busy

This potentially could be one of your better clues. Exponentially the later it is that you call and the line is busy, the higher the probability he is talking to another woman in a romantic manner. If you were to ask him why his telephone line is always busy late-night your going to hear excuses like I'm just talking to my buddies, I've been talking long distance to my mother or I'd been on line on the computer. When a man is sleeping with more than one woman the one constant that must exist is communication. Due to the fact that most woman have a 9 to 5 and a life the most convenient time to talk to the other woman is late at night when her kids are asleep and his other main girlfriend is not around. A late night busy signal implies a late night busy man making plans to do what he thinks he does best. (CHEATING!)

WAY# (74.) <u>Have One Of Your Girlfriends Call Him That He Doesn't Know As Though They Got A Wrong Number</u>

Using her sexiest voice have her call him and ask for someone who doesn't live there. On a third line listen anonymously as your man replies. Have her to complement his voice as sounding like a radio DJ or someone she knows. If your man has cheating ways they will soon manifest themselves, as he will try to take advantage of the situation by initiating more conversation. If he takes the bait your purpose would be better served not to mention what you have heard and done but just make note of the character and morals of the man you are sleeping with.

WAY# (75.) <u>Put A Framed Picture Of You And Him In His Home</u>

Be sure you place it in a specific place in a specific visible position.
Every time you leave his home and come

back check to see if it has been moved. In returning to his home if you find it to be unmoved, you have nothing to worry about. If it has been moved it would only account for one of several explanations.

(1.) There was an earthquake of magnitude 3.5 or better. *(HINT: NOT LIKELY)*

(2.) He was dusting and moved the picture. *(HINT: REALLY UNLIKELY)*

(3.) A flying pig flew in through the window an knocked over the picture. *(HINT: ONLY IF YOUR SMOKING BAD CRACK.)*

(4.) He had another woman over and did not want her to see your picture with him. *(HINT: BINGO!!!)*

NOTE: The larger the picture the better. Cheaters don't like to have anything happen that can spoil the moment when cheating, so a picture of him with another woman would need to be removed.

WAY# (76.) You Have Been Dating For More Than Six Months And Have Not Met His Family

Just short of him being the last living member of the family there is no excuse for this. Even if the family lives out of town you should have been introduced at least by phone. The only other reasoning is that he doesn't feel that you're good enough to meet his family. This should be a red flag that he is not really serious about the relationship or you. A man with good intentions would be proud to introduce you to his family as his lady and would want you to meet his family much sooner rather than later. The real reason you have not met his family is because you're just a fill-in or better stated, he's just filling you up until something better comes along.

WAY# (77.) Men Who Masturbate

Most men would say let he who is not guilty cast the first stone, or should I say nut. Masturbating itself is a form of cheating. By virtue of thinking about other women he can't have and sexual dominance he can't give. This manual release of energy is energy that he will have less of when he has sexual relations with you. In many interviews with men not one said they thought of their current woman doing the act of masturbating. The point was made that the main idea of masturbating was to have other women in a fantasy world that they could never have in reality. About 70% of the men interviewed said that they thought of women that they never had sex with, 30% said they thought of previous girlfriends. This is virtual cheating in 3-D. If he will cheat in the mind he will cheat in the heart and penis.

WAY# (78.) <u>Check His Underwear</u>

If there are shit-stains on the back and front of his underwear the question is not with what woman he is cheating with but what man? If your man leaves out and comes back later than expected.

And you suspect something maybe wrong. Check his underwear for stains as a result of leakage of sperm that can mean one of two things. He has a venereal disease or he's been cheating. Either of which is any good for you. Another clue to look for in his underwear is something called hair transference. That's right, pubic hair during sexual intercourse may be transferred from one person to another which in turn could be found on your man's underwear. If your man's pubic hair is short curly and black and you find a straight blonde strand of hair then you fill in the blanks. Either he's been riding bare back nude on a lion, (LARGE PUSSY) or bare back nude "IN" a blonde woman. (small pussy)

You decide!

WAY# (79.) <u>Find Out The Pass Code To His Answering Service</u>

Underhanded you say, lowdown, trifling, sneaky and un-God like. Well I hope your not looking for an argument. Just refer to the name of this Manifesto or should I say Man-ah-cheat-ho! Now you should be thinking how can I obtain this information. This will be a lot easier than you think. Just learn the location of the numbers on his phone keypad. For example: If the top three numbers going across are (1)--(2)--(3) all you have to do is watch the positioning of his finger when he's ready to dial his pass-code. Look at the movement of the finger and don't try to remember numbers but remember positioning and movement of the finger. If he presses the upper left corner of the phone then you know if has pressed the number (1) and so forth. When you're spending time together in a relationship there will be many opportunities to observe your man using his phone to retrieve his messages.

No one expects someone to be watching

when they dial a phone number, so it will be easy to observe him inconspicuously. The same technique is used to steal bank pin numbers. So you ask how do I know? I watch the Discovery Channel.

WAY# (80.) <u>He Will Not Let You Have A Key To His Apartment Or House</u>

This one may be a little weak in principal but depending how long or serious your relationship is should be taken into consideration. The closer you are the more trust and confidence you should have in one another and if he truly has nothing to hide and has all good intentions then the expectation of having a key to his home is not out of the question. Especially if you have offered him a key to your home and he has not reciprocated. Either he thinks you're a theft or he is sleeping with another woman occasionally and needs his privacy. Ask for his key and listen to his plea.

WAY# (81.) <u>Men Who Don't Like To Make Plans</u>

For a Cheater nothing could be worst than planning time ahead. He like's to keep himself available because he can never be sure of when an opportunity to cheat may present itself. He needs and wants the freedom to make decisions on a day-by-day basis. A cheater will always want to see you on his terms because the very weekend he'll plan to be with you will be the same weekend he could have had a date with someone new. By virtue of him not making plans with you is a sure sign that you are not that important to him. This type of man will be ready to fire excuses at you like a verbal AK-47 as to why he cannot commit to plans ahead of time. If and when he does commit to plans they will often end up as broken promises. The more time you spend with this man the more obvious it becomes that there is a pattern to this behavior. And this pattern fit's a cheater quite well.

WAY# (82.) Hide A Small Sound Activated Tape Recorder In His Bedroom

You are on your own on this one. Due to various laws in various states it may be illegal to record someone without their prior knowledge and consent. Whatever the case may be, you'll find this to be one of the most effective #WAY'S to find out if your man is cheating on you. There are many sizes and disguises of tape recorders that can easily be concealed for recording purposes. They say if you look for trouble you'll find it. So be prepared for the worst.

WAY# (83.) Men Who Come Home And Go Straight To The Shower!

Now keep this in perspective because most men do come home and take a shower. The key here is when they go straight to the shower without doing anything else with little or nothing to say to you.

And then come out of the shower wearing his favorite cologne to mask any possible odors from the other woman. Just on this premise alone is not a reason for alarm. However, couple this with several of other #WAY'S, and they could spell cheater!

WAY# (84.) <u>When Sleeping Together He Stops Cuddling With You</u>

The old cliché actions speak louder than words would apply here. Sometimes it's what we do that's much more profound than what we say. Symbolically as your face can show many different expressions: happiness, confusion, sadness, pain, surprise, anger and so forth. So can your body while in a sleeping position. Now obviously, if you just had an argument, one might expect to sleep in a position that would be different from the norm. But when there is no obvious reason, at least to you, then the most probable cause is guilt.

Because he had sex with another woman last night, or plans on having sex with another woman the next night. As bedtime approaches you'll hear statements like I'm tired as a pre-warning that he doesn't want to be bothered in a sexual manner. This is also supported by the fact that now he's lying on the other side of the bed not touching or cuddling with you. You will also notice him tossing and turning more, getting up in the middle of the night more often, and waking up a lot earlier. Cheating men think mentally they have everything under control. However guilt has a way of manifesting itself through body language that cannot be controlled. Now instead of feeling the strength of his arm around you, the caress of his hand, the throbbing of his penis, the smell of his breath, *(You probably could do without that one!)* there is now only vacant mattress real estate between the two of you. A change in sleep patterns can mean a change of heart! And I don't mean transplant.

WAY # (85.) <u>When The Frequency Of Having Sex Diminishes</u>

In this instance it's safe to say he still enjoys having sex. The question is whom has he started enjoying sex with? This is when bells and whistles should sound along with a hand held raised stop sign! We all like eating and if we stop eating it would be for a reason. Conversely you need to find out why he is now having little or no sex with you. Could it be he suddenly finds the act of sex disgusting and sinful and wants to build a better relationship with God? Or he has started having sex outside of the relationship. Most couples will have a pattern to the frequency of their lovemaking. When this pattern changes for no apparent reason to you, this would be an indicator of the presence of another woman. When a woman offers her body to her man, and he doesn't take it, then the woman should give him a part of her body; Her badly un-pedicured naked right foot with a hang nail, placed sideways up his "Asshole!"

WAY# (86.) <u>When You Visit His Home Check The Phone To See If The Ringer Is On</u>

If you find the ringer in the off position then it becomes obvious he does not want to be bothered while your there. The question is bothered by whom? Nothing could be more uncomfortable than talking on the phone to another woman while your lady is in the same house, let alone the same room. To avoid this scenario a cheater just turns his phone ringer off while you're at his home.

WAY# (87.) <u>When His Phone Rings He Takes The Call In A Different Room</u>

I'm sure if the situation was reversed I know what a man would be thinking........ She's talking to another man. Well it shouldn't be any different when he does it. The assumption would have to be that he is talking about something that he does not want you to hear or know about.
Men for some reason don't see the fault in

doing this. They will defend this action with the premise they are just talking business and you should understand why he needs his privacy. More than likely it is business, monkey business with another woman.

WAY# (88.) <u>Men Who Still Live In The Same Town They Grew Up In</u>

In this case the chances of your man cheating on you go up exponentially with the length of time that he lives in the same town he grew up in. The likelihood of him crossing paths with some girl he grew up with, such as childhood sweetheart's, high school flings, ex-girlfriend's, ex-wives, one night stands, grade school infatuations, X-cheerleaders is not only probable, but inevitable. What could be a greater temptation for a man to cheat? Now that crossed eyed, buck-tooth, knock-knee, overweight, afro-puff wearing on the welfare girl that lived next door to him has blossomed into one of the finest women on planet earth. And when she crosses paths with him some years later, the dog in him will surely bark. Statistically most men will move away from their hometowns by the age of 25. The rest that continue to live in the same hometown will always be haunted by their past. So that 38-year-old man you meet that still lives in the same hometown where he was born and raised will have a higher probability of cheating on you than a man who has moved to a different state.

WAY# (89.) <u>Men Born And Raised In Big Cities</u>

Movie stars, bright light, fast cars, fast women, and fast lifestyles make for little time to grow up in big cities. The key word is exposure! Just by the virtue of a larger population of people in a denser area makes for a more aggressive environment for survival. While growing up with the sight of drug dealers, gangs, prostitutes and pimps become a part of the landscape and makes one learn to eat or be eaten. Fast cities produce fast men with slow morals.

Perhaps this assertion is broad based but has more truth than fiction.

CAPTAIN'S LOG; CHEATING MEN ARE LIKE DIRTY DIAPHERS.........THEY'ER FULL OF SHIT!

WAY# (90.) Men From Dysfunctional Families

Some of the more common traits associated with a dysfunctional family would be physical abuse, drugs, alcoholism, one parent, low income, no education, verbal abuse, low self-esteem, mothers who show no love for their sons, etc., etc., etc. The old saying the fruit does not fall far from the tree would apply here. A man raised in a dysfunctional family will have about as much chance as a one legget man in a ass kicking contest that he will not replicate what he has experienced growing up. As he goes from boyhood to manhood the mental carnage that has accumulated through the years will certainly spring roots and grow at some point during the relationship. Usually in the form of a hostile attitude with little or no respect for the relationship. Cheating on you becomes a form of abuse he uses to express his anger and without professional help he can't change the cycle of mental oppression and cheating.

WAY# (91.) <u>Have Your Man Take A Polygraph Test</u>

If you suspect you're man of cheating then confront him with this suspicion by asking him to take a polygraph test to relieve any doubt. All you have to do is call 1-877-POLY TEST and leave your information or fax 24 hours a day at (570) 223-7265. This is available all over the country and can be done in your home for nominal fee. Any man with nothing to hide would submit to this to prove his dedication and love only to you. If he's cheating on you he would sooner walk through a Lions cage with the pork chop tied around his neck before submitting to such a test. The only drawback to this technique is that he may then want you to take a polygraph test.

WAY# (92.) Purchase A Semen Detection Kit

Yes, yes, "let's find out what's really going on". The quick and easy way with the Check Mate Semen Detection Kit. You can detect invisible traces of semen in his underwear. By reason of you reading this Manifesto you must be filled with suspicion and doubt caused by your man's infidelity. With the Semen Detection Test Kit you can easily monitor your man's sexual activity outside of the relationship by detecting invisible traces of dried semen that is left in his underwear after sex!

The five-minute test is simply the easiest and most cost-effective way to put an end to the nightmare of suspicion and doubt caused by a cheating man.

Most users of this test will be interested in testing articles thought to have only recently been soiled, however traces of dried semen will remain present for long periods of time.

As long as your article to be tested has not been washed, invisible traces of dried semen can easily be detected for up to two years or longer.

You can be sure if any traces of semen are present on the area you decide to test, it will find even the smallest trace amounts. The patent pending Check Mate Infidelity Test Kit is guaranteed to detect it.

Your man brings evidence home to you without even knowing it. A man will continue to secrete small amounts of semen for up to two hours or more after each sexual encounter.

Even if your man uses a condom during sexual intercourse there will still be traces of his semen in his underwear. Of course when confronted with this evidence, you will here excuses like: I masturbated, I watched an X-rated movie over my buddies house and got a hard-on, or I was at a topless bar and got too excited.

You will hear weak excuses but you will have strong evidence.

What else would you expect him to say when confronted with the truth? Everyone's situation is different. So if your man leaves the house and says he's going to Church that afternoon and you check his underwear that evening and find traces of semen what is he going to say? I got the Holly-Ghost and came on myself! PLEASE! A woman's intuition combine with an easy-to-use home test kit make for one complete investigation.

To purchase contact---<u>The Spy Chest:</u>

Phone/ (850) 683-8787

Fax/ (850) 682-0083

Web site/ checkmate.htm

WAY# (93.) Place A Hidden Camera In His Bedroom

Miniature stealthy video cameras can be very easily hidden Inside of a wall clock, smoke detector, radio, book, ink pen, just to mention a few. The only thing more convincing than hearing what your man is doing would be to see what your man is doing. Wireless camera systems will allow you to do this quite easily. This technique should certainly answer your most burning questions about fidelity of your man. Be mentally prepared for what you might see because it may raise more questions than answers. Like whom is that man getting in bed with my man????

Go on line to the Spy Chest for more details about their hidden surveillance cameras at www.spytechs.com .

Or call (850) 683-8787.

WAY# (94.) <u>Place A GPS Vehicle Tracking System On His Car</u>

GPS is short for global positioning system. GPS tracking systems are satellite-based navigation systems. This data can be used for personal tracking of your man 24 hours a day 7 days a week. So if you have any doubt about where your man says he is going or where he has been. GPS tracking devices will allow you to find the truth for yourself. The only Colbert action you will need to do is find a reason to borrow his car to have the system installed. Then you only need to match where he says he's going to where you know he has been. Now when he tells you he has to work late you will know specifically where he's working. The question is whom is he working on?

<u>Contact</u>: Spy Chest for more information.
Web site: <u>www.spytechs.com</u>
Phone: (850) 683-8787

WAY# (95.) Purchase A Telephone Recording System

You may secretly record both sides of a conversation with a telephone-recording device available from the Spy Chest. It doesn't matter how many phones there are in the house or what room there located in. A monitor option allows you to listen to conversations as you record them. Its compact size makes the recorder easily concealed and portable. Now let's think about this for a moment......you suspect your husband or boyfriend of cheating and if true he will surely communicate to this person by phone. Now you have the ability to listen to these conversations for verification to what you have suspected. You won't need a judge and jury to wait for the verdict on this one. As seeing is to believing, hearing is to knowing. If he speaks no evil, you will hear no evil. Check with your state and local laws for usage.

Contact: Spy Chest (850) 683-8787
Web site: www.spytechs.com

WAY# (96.) Use A Voice Changer

You will certainly have a lot of fun with this one. (Also available from Spy Chest)

This device offers 8 different voices with altering settings that makes your natural voice not be recognized. Now you can be whomever you want to be, or whoever you want your man to think you are and listen to the true character of the man you are with. Just let your imagination be your guide. *Also good for calling into work sick!*

WAY# (97.) Have A Background Check Done On Your Man

This can easily be accomplished by contacting a company called: U.S. Information Search Inc.

Phone: (800) 596-4327

The following services would be available giving specific Information regarding your man.

*State criminal records search
*County criminal records search

*Education verification (double check this one)
*Driving records search
*Social Security number trace
*Credit report (triple check this one)
*Medical records and much more.
If you uncover lies in any of these areas then surely there's a lot more. Like who was he really with the night he said he was out with the fellows?

WAY# (98.) Hire A Surveillance Agency To Follow Your Man

If you have a legitimate suspicion of your man cheating on you, you may have him followed, watched, and videotaped. This may be considered to be a bit extreme for only a suspicion but you can't put a price tag on your peace of mind. If this is what it takes to confirm or deny your suspicions than it is money well spent. Simply call **Rocky Mountain Security Agency.**

Phone: (303) 817-4473

E-mail: JVF@1RMSA.COM

WWW: 1rmsa.com

WAY# (99.) Call A Professional Decoy Agency

Professional female model decoys can be used to test your boyfriend or husbands fidelity. The agency uses very attractive females of all races and ages to see if your potential husband or current husband will cheat on you. (As seen on TV.) You'll have the option of going along to observe or viewing the video to see the results for yourself. **Contact Rocky Mountain security agency:**

Phone: 1-(877) 312-2766
E-mail: JVF@1RMSA.COM
WWW: 1rmsa.com

WAY# (100.) MEN Who Have Been To Bachelor Parties

In my many interviews with men of all ages and races regarding this subject (Bachelor parties) I've listened to some of the most unbelievable acts and situations you could imagine.

The information for the most part was even shocking to me! And I thought I had been to some wild bachelor parties. As the story was told. The groom along with his male married friends, men engaged, and men in steady relationships behaving like a pack of wild dogs in heat. I guess there's a lot to be said about peer pressure here but mixing alcohol, naked dancing women and loud music together in a room full of men are the ingredients for sure submission of any morals, inhibitions and commitment to love ones. Everything is in jeopardy. The fact of the matter is it doesn't matter how strong wield the man is, or even to what degree a man may think he will not participate in anything sexual. He is guilty by association. The fact that he's even there to see, hear and smell make him a cheater. I was told a story about a man who was the brother of the groom who was happily married, committed to his wife and a minister of a church. He wanted nothing to do with what was going on at the bachelor party.

But the men who were there convinced him that It was the first Sunday of the month and it would be ok to have a glass of wine for communion. But then the fellows got him to have another glass of wine, followed by another and another to the point he passed out only to be awakened by a hooker with his penis in her mouth! As the story goes, he did not resist. I guess the moral of the story is association brings stimulation, not simulation.

WAY# (101.) <u>MEN Who Take Viagra</u>

Now with the ability to achieve what I call a mechanical erection. Man's confidence and performance along with his penis has risen to new highs (Literally). With this new felt confidence comes a seek and conquer mentality towards women. The wife or girlfriend cannot keep up with their man's newfound sexual energy making him more lightly to cheat on you.

This newfound confidence in a cheating man gives him an insatiable sexual appetite that needs to be feed frequently by any woman who will let him eat.

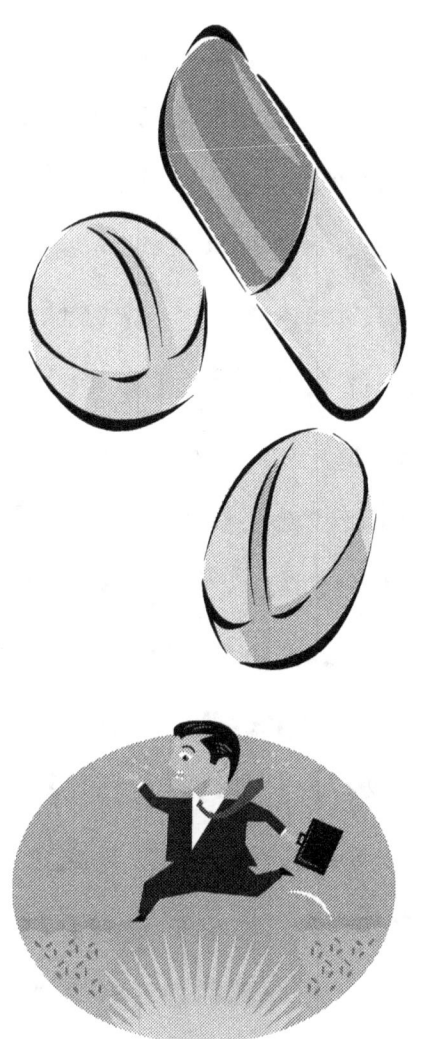

Captain's Commentary

Congratulations to those of you who had the courage to complete this voyage of truth! This mental Cruise Ship has now safely docked and the ramp of reality has been lowered for your safe exiting. Now that you're back on dry land and you have rejoined society. Pass the word on about your vacation cruise of truth to all women that you come in contact with. My goal as your Captain is to let all women know the "Truth" Is out there. No, not hidden away in some X-Files in area 51, But in my Manifesto that can easily be ordered.

To be straight to the point there's too much emphasis on sex in our society today that has led to the decline of morals that affects every aspect of our lives. Our children are being exposed to sexual corruption at a very young age and it never stops. Aggressively and progressively we as a society are being desensitize over the act of sex and nudity.

Sexual connotations are used in every form of advertising. At present day there seemingly cannot be a movie made without the image of a model like woman with her breast & ass being exposed in a sexual manner with no rhyme or reason to the content of the movie. Other than the logic of, if we put a beautiful woman in this movie and show her naked somewhere in the movie, it will somehow be a blockbuster hit! As my father always told me there is a time and place for everything. If I were going to movies to watch the Invasion of Aliens on Earth, then my expectations would be to see good special effects of aliens invading earth, not some woman's Size 38D breast in a love scene which has no correlation to the content of the movie. The entire movie industry seems to make it a point to expose some part of woman's body in a sexual manner no matter what the movie is about. The same argument can be made for regular TV as well. The only difference is that it's more suggestive on television than visual.

You will find this to even be true on Saturday morning cartoons or any day thereafter. Just try watching some cartoons with your kids and see just how sexually suggestive they are. Long legs, short dresses, breast, and excess makeup on young animated faces just to point out a few. I don't care what media it is. Internet, magazines, radio, newspapers, billboards, videos, and everything else you can think of. Sex, sex, sex, and more sex! It's no wonder that the institution of marriage has declined to what it is today. That's right, same sex marriages and divorce rates higher than ever before. Whether you are aware of this or not men are programmed to cheat at very young ages. Due to the high commercialism of young women's bodies which only stimulate a boy's sexuality and not his morality. Ironic that after the male comes out of a vagina at birth, he spends the rest of his life trying to get back into one. There is an argument to be made when God created Adam he was the first man he ever made.

Sort of a demo or test model if you will. And "mistakes" were made. God forgot to connect Adams penis to his heart and brains. When God created Eve he corrected these error's. This is why a man's penis has developed it's own line of reasoning and thinking because of being totally disconnected from the "Big Brain" and heart. Through evolution Mr. Penis has developed a small brain in the head of the penis without a heart, although it learned to pulsate like one. Unfortunately this small brain does not generate enough electrical current to break the flat line on a electro-Dick-a-gram.

Women just can't understand the dilemma of being a penis. As your CAPTAIN of "Truth" I will explain it to you. Due to Gods lack of engineering experience in the penis he created a penis with only one eye it can't see out of, his closest relative is a ass hole, his only friend is a pussy, and he has to hang around two hairy nut's 24 hours a day, and every time he stands up for very long he throws up.

Mr. Penis (ADAM) & Miss fidelity (EVE) have been at odds since the beginning of time due to Gods engineering error's in Man's DICK. (AKA Penis)

For you atheists out there an argument can be made for evolution as well. Even before man was walking upright there was no purpose or advantage in being with only one mate. Actually it was quite the contrary. The more woman he mates with the higher the probability his genes will be pasted on to ensure the perpetuation of the race. It is through these primitive motives that modern man unconsciously functions today. Genetically men are engineered and programmed to CHEAT. Early woman on the other hand looked for a more stable environment with a big strong man who is most likely to provide for and protect her kids. Making her less likely to cheat. The only animal early woman needed was man. Now modern day women need four animals. A Mink coat on her back, a Jaguar in her garage, a Tiger in bed, and a "Jackass" to pay for it all.

Even the epidemic of AIDS has not slowed down the tide of cheaters throughout the world. It is my position that mankind needs to be sexually put in check. And with the information presented in my Manifesto this can be accomplished. Conversely, just like men don't rob banks *(Most of them)* for fear of being caught. So will the cheating men of the planet. My legacy in life will be to accomplish what God and society hasn't. A population of men who won't cheat on their women. To honor and celebrate this fact, I hereby decree April 15, National Cheaters Day. Symbolic to all the cheaters on their taxes. This will be a day for all Cheaters (Man or Woman) to go out to a nightclub or bar and celebrate! Standup to be counted for what you are......not what you pretend to be. Confess the fact that you are a cheating lowlife and celebrate new beginnings with a drink of Southern Comfort and Coke. SCC for short. *(Sinful Cheaters Changed).*

GOOD LUCK TO YOU ALL!
YOUR CAPTAIN

CAPTAIN'S PRAYER FOR CHEATING MEN

JESUS on a CROSS! By the power of CHRIST I compel thee. Ye Ole Serpent of EVIL! I bind you in the BLOOD of JESUS you lustful Demon Of Sin. Raise up and OUT of the souls, minds, and "penis" of cheating men. And by the power of my words I command and demand you DEMON! Back to the deepest, darkest, Pitts of HELL'S FIRE.

*"PoOOF" ! be Gone DEMON!!!
*(REPEAT THIS 3 TIMES)

From the voice of Redemption, I confess all the ways of Cheating Men to be exposed, and banished from their minds, heart and souls in the name of JESUS!

Through this prayer may all cheating men be Exorcized by the power vested in this Manifesto. Ashes to Ashes, Dust to Dust, a cheating man you can never trust!

AAAAA MEN.

CAPTAIN'S MEN COMMANDMENTS

I.

THOU SHALT HAVE NO OTHER WOMEN

II.

THOU SHALT NOT BEAR FALSE INTENTIONS

III.

THOU SHALT NOT USE THY WOMENS NAME IN VAIN

IV.

THOU SHALT REMEMBER ALL ANNIVERSARIES AND BIRTHDAYS

V.

HONOR THY WIFE, OR GIRLFRIEND

VI.
THOU SHALT NOT KILL! THY WIFE OR GIRLFRIED
VII.
THOU SHALT NOT COMMIT EVIL ACTS AGAINST THY WOMEN
IX.
THOU SHALT NOT BEAR FALSE WITNESS AGAINST FEMALE NEIGHBORS
X.
THOU SHALT NOT LUST FOR OTHER WOMEN, THAN HIS OWN

CAPTAIN'S CHEATER PETER METER CHART

Put a check mark next to the #WAY that applies to you and give it a rating between 1 thru 5, five being worst possible scenario for each one checked. Then do your totals for points. Giving a point value of 1 for each #WAY checked. Also total point value for 1 thru 5 ratings column and add these two totals together and fine your corresponding rating interpretation.

#WAYS √ LIST   1 TO 5   NOTES

1.)_____

2.)_____

3.)_____

4.)_____

5.)_____

6.)_____

7.)_____

#WAYS √ LIST   1 TO 5   NOTES

8.)_____

9.)_____

10.)_____

11.)_____

12.)_____

13.)_____

14.)_____

15.)_____

16.)_____

17.)_____

18.)_____

19.)_____

20.)_____

21.)_____

22.)_____

23.)_____

24.)_____

25.)_____

26.)_____

27.)_____

28.)_____

29.)_____

30.)_____

31.)_____

#WAYS √ LIST   1 TO 5   NOTES

32.)_____

33.)_____

34.)_____

35.)_____

36.)_____

37.)_____

38.)_____

39.)_____

40.)_____

41.)_____

42.)_____

43.)_____

44.)_____

45.)_____

46.)_____

47.)_____

48.)_____

49.)_____

50.)_____

51.)_____

52.)_____

53.)_____

54.)_____

55.)_____

#WAYS √ LIST   1 TO 5   NOTES

56.)_____

57.)_____

58.)_____

59.)_____

60.)_____

61.)_____

62.)_____

63.)_____

64.)_____

65.)_____

66.)_____

67.)_____

68.)_____

69.)_____

70.)_____

71.)_____

72.)_____

73.)_____

74.)_____

75.)_____

76.)_____

77.)_____

78.)_____

79.)_____

#WAYS √ LIST   1 TO 5   NOTES

80.)_____

81.)_____

82.)_____

83.)_____

84.)_____

85.)_____

86.)_____

87.)_____

88.)_____

89.)_____

90.)_____

91.)_____

92.)_____

93.)_____

94.)_____

95.)_____

96.)_____

97.)_____

98.)_____

99.)_____

100.)_____

101.)_____

@ SEE CHEATER PETER METER

CONVERSION CHART FOR RATINGS >>>>>>

1 TO 5 RATINGS

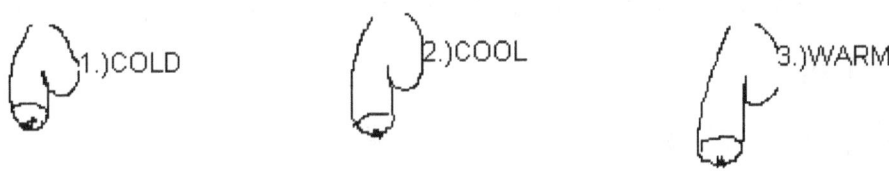

1.)COLD   2.)COOL   3.)WARM

___ - ___ - ___

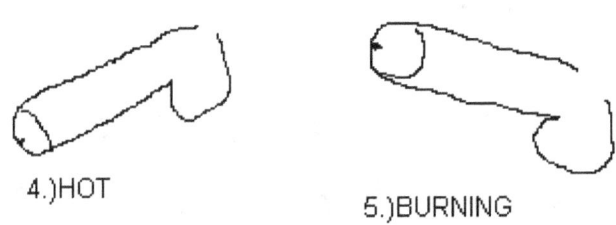

4.)HOT   5.)BURNING

TOTAL POINTS RATINGS

1 TO 49 = GOOD GUY BASICALLY. THIS IS A KEEPER. TAKE HIM HOME TO MEET MOMA. DON'T LEAVE HIM ALONE WITH YOUR GIRLFRIENDS AND YOU WILL DO JUST FINE.

50 TO 99 = WANTS TO BE A GOOD GUY. WILL ONLY CHEAT IF THE WOMAN IS PURSUING HIM. CLOSER COMMUNICATION WILL CORRECT THE PROBLEM. EVEN IN YOUR PRESENCE DON'T HAVE HIM AROUND YOUR GIRLFRIENDS.

100 TO 149 = CURRENTLY THINKING ABOUT CHEATING ON YOU. HAS PLAYBOY LIKE TENDENCIES ALTHOUGH HE THINKS HE'S DOING NOTHING WRONG. COUNSELING TOGETHER WITH PRAYER AND A DIP IN HOLLY WATER MAY HELP BUT NOT LIKELY.

150 TO 200 = THIS IS A SUPER CHEATER! HE'S PROABILY HAVING SEX WITH ANOTHER WOMAN WHILE YOUR READING THIS. THIS IS A HO, GIGOLO AND SLUT ALL ROLLED TOGETHER. DUMP HIM! REHABILITATION IS NOT POSSIBLE. HE WILL GO TO HELL AND STILL BE A HO!

OVER 200 = THIS IS A PIMP OR WANT TO BE PIMP. AS FAR AS HE'S CONCERNED YOU'RE JUST ANOTHER PIECE OF MEAT IN HIS MEAT MARKET. HE ONLY SEE'S YOU FOR: (WHAT HAVE YOU DONE FOR ME LATELY.) RUN DON'T WALK AWAY FROM THIS MAN AND CUT YOUR LOSSES.

www.ingramcontent.com/pod-product-compliance
Lightning Source LLC
Chambersburg PA
CBHW080414290526
45791CB00008BA/2265